<u>PREFACE</u>

This book is not a step by step guide to living off the grid. It is; however, a guide to cause creative thinking with the task of off-grid living in mind. By no means is any of the content intended to be fool proof and 100% accurate, for living off the grid is an all gray area. Nothing is set in stone except that each day will end, and there is always tomorrow.

Society seems to have lost the ability to think "outside the box" and many cannot settle on a true definition of "off-grid" living. Arguments rage, yet there is a most simplistic answer:

"LIVING OFF-GRID IS WHAT EVER DEFINITION YOU DECIDE"

Let no man judge another, for it is inside the soul that decides one's own peace and fulfillment.

CONTENTS

THE DECISION

So you find yourself sitting behind your desk, or performing some dull remedial job task, and constantly thinking about how your life could be better, or at least simpler. The constant battle of life vs. material items weighs on your mind, and you wonder if there is any end in sight. Bills come and go as you continue with the daily struggle of survival, yet you find yourself wondering if you are truly happy, or just passing through this life subservient of its demands. The daily "routine" has now became an excruciating trial of your will.

You sit at your kitchen table, or on the sofa, and stir the food on your plate, wondering exactly what it is that you are consuming. Your eyes are glued to a television that either displays a new trend movie, or spits the so-called "news" from its speakers. You perform your daily ritual of life, and settle into bed to only awaken to perform the same function tomorrow. As you fade off into slumber your last thoughts are of reaching some type of compromise; some type of satisfaction; some type of internal peace.

You are not alone. Many people in modern society are just tired of the direction their life is headed. They yearn for something different. They yearn to return to some semblance of their Grandparents time; a time that seemed simpler and more rewarding. You stop and ponder for a moment and then reach the conclusion that something must change and today is the day that the change will take place. Almost immediately you are filled with a feeling of relaxation and comfort.

To begin your journey you must remember one thing throughout the entire process…"You are trying to leave the stress and chaos behind…Do not make the transition to a simpler life stressful and chaotic!" "One day at a time", and "one simple step at a time" are wonderful words to live by.

I have been there, and I have already made the basic mistakes of making the transition to a simpler life. Take heed as I am trying to ease the burden placed upon you. Life is complicated, but it does not have to be. Yes, modern times exhaust even the most prepared soul, and society seems to have a way of being fickle about any matter. Your goal now is to change your lifestyle. To change the inner turmoil that seems to have consumed you. Trust me when I say it is all about stopping to take a deep breath and a simple change in mindset. Hope is just around the corner.

I hear on a daily basis arguments of the true definition of "off-grid living." If you cast yourself into the judgmental elements of society…then you will have a black and white definition. Everybody these days wants to slander, and destroy one's happiness. Everybody has an opinion, and some believe that only their opinion counts. Wrong!

YOU determine, and you alone, what your style of off-grid living is. Whether it be in an apartment and simply growing vegetables in the window, or living in the remote wilderness with no neighbors for miles – it truly is your personal decision and it doesn't matter what anyone says.

If you have trouble with separating yourself from public opinion, then may I suggest you stand in front of a mirror and practice saying, "I do not care what you think" repeatedly.

This decision is about you, and what is best for you (and your family if applicable). Unfortunately there is an element of society who prides themselves in destroying people's dreams and desires, and are relentless in their attacks.

You must sever these people from your life...it doesn't matter what they feel, believe, or want. This is not about them. Once this has been achieved...now you can continue the process of living a more rewarding and peaceful life.

Now I want you to take out a piece of paper and a pen. Write down what it is that you seek, and what you intend to do in order to achieve this. Also scribble down what your definition of "off-grid living" is. Now look at what you wrote. Compare the writings and begin constructing on paper how you believe you can intertwine these items. Lastly, begin your journey and start accomplishing what you have wrote.

Many people just want a more relaxing lifestyle, or more nutritious food for their family. Many want to completely sever mankind and desire only to be left alone. No matter where you fall onto the scale, your goals can be achieved with a little creative thinking and ambition. If you have a spouse, both must be willing to participate, and both must agree to each change. Never assume that your spouse will agree...always ask.

Now take a look around your house, apartment, whatever you reside in. How much clutter do you have? How much are you willing to live without? How much is really necessary for you to survive? How much are you willing to sacrifice if you want to live in a remote cabin in the woods, or an RV, or simply a smaller apartment? Are you going to remain employed, or are you striving to be debt free and attempt a sustenance lifestyle?

Material items truly have consumed our lives. Believe it or not, you can survive with only 3% of the usual material items found in a home. As I have stated, it's all about what you want and desire. Downsize accordingly.

Once you have made your final decision, it is time to act. Try and do one thing every day that guides you towards your ultimate goal. This will prevent frustration, and yet accomplish a needed task. Nothing happens overnight, so I caution you to not expect it to. The transition will occur, and it is best to do so when you are prepared.

These items to accomplish daily can be as simple as placing canned goods into a plastic tub for later use, or placing $1.00 into the land fund. It can be reading about hydroponics, or clearing out the east facing window sill to begin growing your own herbs. Make it fun...whatever it is. Always remember that making this transition is to be fun with only minimal stress, if any.

I highly recommend practicing your desired new lifestyle prior to making the transition. Do as you would off-grid.

THE LAND

If you have decided to move onto your own piece of land, then this chapter will provide some guidelines and suggestions for obtaining it. Based on your initial decisions, you now have a major goal to achieve. Things that you must ask yourself are "Am I going to stay employed to support a land payment?" "Do I save and purchase land outright?" "Is land available near my employment?" "How much land do I really need?"

The best land for someone interested in off-grid living is raw land, or recreational land. These properties usually are located in remote areas, and can require creativity in order to reach them. Shop for your land. There are many properties available, and only you can determine what will suffice your needs. I suggest the largest plot that you can afford to allow for privacy and sustainable living. An acre is sufficient, but offers only minimal privacy.

Ensure that you research zoning regulations prior to purchasing your land. That is why it is suggested to look at recreational and raw land. The last thing you want to happen is a zoning regulation preventing you from residing on your land as you desire. Do your Due Diligence!

Do what you can afford.

I'm a very private person and require space. I also enjoy hunting and fishing; therefore, my piece of paradise has a stocked pond and is over 5 acres. It's partially wooded, but offers grass fields for livestock, and also has a small river that runs along the backside of the property.

Nothing says to be off-grid you must totally isolate yourself and eat tree bark. Nothing says that you cannot purchase your land and pull an RV on the property to live in. Maybe you choose to build your own log cabin. Maybe you choose to live in a tent. The possibilities are endless as long as it makes you happy.

<u>SHELTER & SUCH</u>

This is a topic that seems to frustrate people the most. You're going to need some type of shelter so why let it be such a stressful event? Here is where that downsizing comes into play. If you don't need it to survive…then you probably don't need it at all. Many people attempt to overload a small living structure and that's where the problems begin. If you are cramped up inside a 12 x 12 cabin, how are you going to be happy?

Again, this involves individual needs and affordability. Many storage shed venders offer wonderful alternative cabins on a rent to own basis. You can either purchase outright, or make an affordable monthly payment. It's all in how you decide you want your lifestyle to be.

Maybe you want to build your own cabin from the trees located on the property you have purchased? Many versions of chainsaw mills are now available for low cost so this can be an option. Absolutely nothing says that you cannot live in a tent. Some people prefer tent living due to the low cost and versatility factors. I do caution you to have a well thought out plan for heating during the winter months. I have seen a simple wood framed shed with a woodstove inside, attached to the tent, provide sufficient heating during the winter months. Let you imagination be endless!

I chose a simple cabin shell and decided to finish off the interior myself. One day at a time and one step at a time, it now has been completed. For those that like to be frugal, many building materials can be obtained for free on Craigslist or from construction sites - all you have to do is ask if you can have them.

A shelter can be as unique and expensive, or as inexpensive, as you desire. All of them provide one thing...and one thing only...protection from the elements. Once shelter is obtained you now can embark on making wonderful memories, and expanding your homestead.

Simple, or not, life off-grid is truly an adventure.

<u>NO STRESS TRANSITION</u>

You now have your land and have selected a shelter and gotten it onto the proerty. Now you have decisions as to how you are going to live, such as with/without electricity? Running water? Water source? Lighting?

These can be overwhelming, but again, with a non-stressful outlook; creativity, and ambition – nothing is impossible. Many alternatives exist for the modern day off-gridder. Some are as simple as filling water jugs and carrying them into your property. Others are as complex as drilling a well and installing electric, or solar panels, to operate the pump.

First, decide whether you will live with, or without, electricity. Research shows that normal exposure to breaker boxes, and electricity are not the best conditions for your body, but this is totally up to you. Running electricity to a remote property will be very expensive.

An alternative, and my preference, is solar power and/or a generator. Inexpensive, yet provides electricity to a high degree of comfort. Water wheels are also an option with a hydro pump. You will be surprised as to how little electricity is required to power only needed items, instead of the modern conveniences that promote serving the corporate structure.

You will especially start to monitor your water consumption once it becomes your responsibility to carry it in to your property.

<u>THE NEEDS OF THE FEW</u>

If you have been performing daily tasks towards your transition to off-grid, then you are way ahead of the game. Downsizing should already have taken place, if not, prepare yourself for one huge garage sale. Below is a list of what I find necessary for off-grid living: The list is as follows:

Propane Stove/Wood Stove – Heating & Meal preparation

Lighting – Solar powered bulbs

Generator – Charging batteries and immediate power

Solar System – provides power for small television, radio, DVD player, portable refrigerator, and fans.

Tools – Ax, Hammer, Saw, Nails, etc.

Kitchen Items – Pots/Pans, Dishes, Silverware, Glasses, etc.

Bedding

Clothes

Toiletries

5 Gallon Buckets – Get as many as you can.

As you can see...it's a small list. You don't need the 83" Big Screen, Dishwasher, Side by Side Refrigerator, and so on. Simple tends to mean more time for living outdoors, daily chores, and quality family time. Outdoor time becomes much more meaningful and enjoying, as opposed to playing a video game in front of the television.

You decide your off-grid experience...and only you. You decide if you have a television, radio, kerosene lights, or otherwise. You decide if you are going to have a greenhouse, livestock, and other animals. Make it is simple, or complex as you like.

The key to living a less stressful life is keeping it simple. The simpler your life is...the less stress and chaos you will have. When fulfilling the basic needs is all you have to think about, life becomes less complicated and more focused. You know what needs to be done, and you will achieve great daily satisfaction by accomplishing it.

Nothing is more rewarding than feeding yourself with the bounty that you have grown yourself, or hunted. All the work pays off in that first bite. You know where it came from and you know that it is safe for your family to eat. No chemicals, just a little labor of love. Suddenly all of those material items will not mean so much.

DAILY LIFE

If you have decided to move onto your land and have sought a simpler lifestyle, your daily agenda will change considerably. No longer will you concentrate on the trials of meeting the demands of society, but rather on the basics of survival. Watering plants and the garden; chopping wood; gathering wood if you cook with a wood stove; tending animals; fixing a leak in the roof; and so forth are now your priorities. Do you know what meshes right into these daily tasks? Spending quality time with loved ones, of course. In my experience, there is no replacement for the bond that is constructed while living off-grid.

If you remain employed, but live off-grid, these daily tasks will still be required, but possibly to a lesser degree. Time management will come into play, but it depends on your arrangement as to if all gets accomplished as required.

Daily life for those that are trying to be self-sufficient will be met with daily requirements. If you procrastinate...you might not eat. Leaving it for tomorrow...you might not bathe. Putting it off until next week...your roof might cave in. By no means am I saying that off-grid life must be hectic. Nope...but it must be met with responsibility and persistence. Off-grid life is not easy. You will work hard, but the benefits are priceless.

THE DINNER TABLE

What you eat for dinner is totally dependent on you. If you are living remotely it won't be as simple as calling the pizza delivery service. One thing that I found to really, really assist with this venture is to begin stockpiling food during the initial decision making process. I chose to vacuum seal consumables and placed these in 5 gallon buckets. I also began to buy extra canned goods, canned meats, beans, etc. In no time you will have accumulated a year's supply of food. Use one year as your goal to collect. What that means is for one year you will not be required to worry about food supply, and this will give you ample time to prepare and accumulate during the initial off-grid transition.

I highly recommend that you begin researching how to grow your own food supply. This can be done year round by using a simple Kratky Hydroponics system. I also dare say, that a greenhouse is a must. There are many examples scattered throughout the internet, and each is easily heated with a little ingenuity during the cold months. I also highly recommend researching and learning how to preserve fresh vegetables, fruits, and meat. Every item you grow will cut your food expense, and provide a wonderful feeling of self-reliability.

Hunting and fishing will also provide a source of meat, and I recommend doing so as much as possible. A good rule of thumb while living off-grid is you will need 140 days of meat to survive the winter months. Any addition to your food supply during the warm months will only make this easier during the cold months. Again, having a supply of food already built up only eases this burden.

I encourage building food plots for wildlife on your property, and also raising domestic livestock. Chickens are an invaluable source of food, and raising hens is so much fun! Goats are my favorite and provide a meat and dairy source, plus the fact that they are little lawn mowers on hooves. One can do beef cattle for butcher, and never forget about Mr. Oinker. Butchering a hog yourself is quite easy, and nothing takes the place of fresh bacon. You will need to have the means to freeze the excess pork, but again this can be done with ingenuity and resourcefulness.

 Are you starting to see the bigger picture yet? It all boils down to you determining your existence. If you want pork…raise pork. If you want fish…catch fish. If you want venison…deer hunt. Eggs…raise chickens. You will find that the Circle of Life will begin to play out on your homestead. Raise corn to feed chickens and animals, etc.

There truly is no replacement for living a simpler life. In only a short time you will have completely forgotten about modern conveniences and the hustle and bustle you once were caught up in.

As a means to provide cooling of foods off-grid, I offer the above photograph of a Zeer Pot. These work wonderfully, and can maintain cold temps even on the hottest days of summer. This is one means of preserving your gardens bounty, and will only cost you the price of the materials needed to make. I highly recommend research of this item, and it's utilization on those of you that do not have the means for an electrical source.

Being very easy to construct, you will need two clay pots (one larger than the other). Simply place the smaller pot inside the larger one and fill gap between the two pots with sand. Wet the side and cover the top with a towel. Watch as the interior temperature drops due to natural condensation. It's that simple.

WATER BY THE GALLON

The title explains it all. You will find that most people totally abuse the water supply. There will no longer be hour long showers; letting the faucet run for no apparent reason; filling the tub to the top; washing fifteen items separately.

You will learn to appreciate every gallon of water that you use, especially if you are carrying it in to your homestead. Water will be conserved naturally, and you will find that there is no need for excessive use. Drinking, cooking, bath time, and laundry time are the primary times of need. You will also need a water supply for your livestock, and pets.

I recommend a rainwater collection system as it offers ability to collect water for other than drinking purposes. A collection system is easily constructed from 55 gallon plastic barrels, and provides a constant supply of water as long as it rains. Pumping this into your house, or to a barn is easily done with an inexpensive solar water pump.

Bathing can be conducted using minimal water, and choices are that of a tub or a tank less water heater. Gravity will provide sufficient pressure for use of a tank less water heater, and hot water is instantaneous. If not using a tank less water heater, its back to the boil and carry method.

I have one simple solution for providing safe drinking water – BOIL IT.

THE CHANGING SEASONS

Every season has its own set of challenges and only time will show you what these are in your particular area. Spring brings rain showers and possible flooding with thunderstorms. Spring also brings tornadoes which for those off-grid requires extra [preparation. You must have a way to power a weather radio to alert you about pending danger.

 Summer brings an entire new meaning to those that rely on air conditioning. Air conditioning can be obtained by means of using a generator, or solar power, or one can settle for use of fans. Fans can provide relative comfort during the hot summer months, but I'll leave this to your imagination and creativity to come up with your cooling preference. Summer also brings out all the squirmy, flying, squiggly, biting, slithering pests that Mother Nature has to offer. Study up and be aware of what presents itself in your area. Scorpions are not fun to deal with, neither are snakes.

Fall is a wonderful time of year for off-grid living. Cooler temperatures, and change of leaf colors, creates a nostalgic mindset and provides a much needed break from the summer heat. Last minute fall crops can be gathered and planted, and preparations for winter crops made. Fall is also hunting season so harvesting meat is essential.

Winter can be either a fun time, if you are prepared, or a nightmare. Depending on your area, temperatures can plummet for weeks at a time, and survival comes down to food stockpiles; feed for your livestock, and wood supply. If you did not cut enough firewood prior to winter, it now will be a major chore. Any shortage in the aforementioned areas is not easily rectified. My suggestion for winter is PREPARE...PREPARE...PREPARE.

Consume a lot of protein during the winter months as you will need it. I highly recommend stews and soups made from your home grown vegetables, with addition of whatever type of meat you desire. These warm the body, and provide necessary nutrients for survival. There is nothing better than entering a home from the cold, and smelling the wonderful scent of a boiling stew.

BEEF or VENISON STEW RECIPE

Deeply brown meat in oil.

Add onions, garlic, Worcestershire sauce, oregano, salt, and water.

Simmer covered for 1 ½ to 2 hours, or until meat is tender.

Add potatoes, carrots; cook until tender.

Combine flour and water – Stir into stew.

ENJOY!

Wood most likely will be your cost-effective source of heat, but do not forget about propane. Relatively cheap, propane can be used to supplement wood heat. IT also provides immediate heat in the mornings when the stove burns out, and you did not awake to put more wood on the fire. This will happen, so keep this in mind.

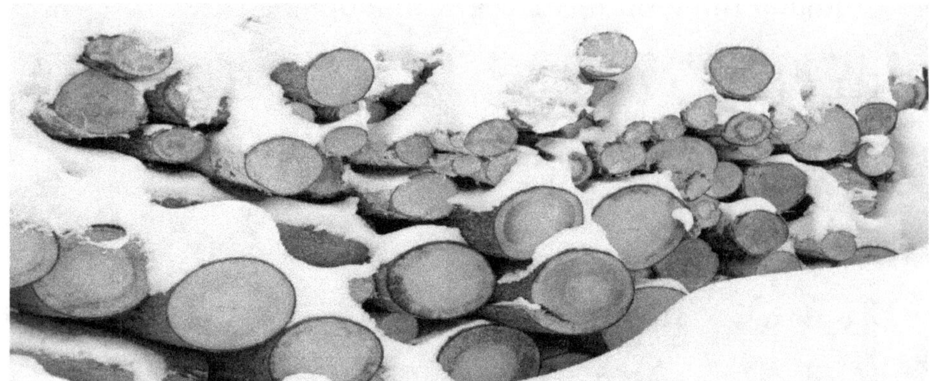

Some people get caught up in the size of the wood to burn. Frankly, cut to the size of your stove and what you can carry. Why strain yourself handling a huge log when you can add two smaller logs and get the same result? Some like chainsaws...I prefer a bow saw just because I learned to appreciate every log, and what Mother Nature has provided. I also enjoy the listening to the sounds of nature, and the buzz of a chainsaw deters from this enjoyment.

Always try and cut more than what you think you will need. It can always be used the following year. There is nothing more frustrating than to look at your wood pile in January and see only three or four remaining logs, and it is snowing. Cutting wood in the snow is not the most enjoyable experience.

Never forget that during the winter months that the fish also are biting. Though a totally different manner of fishing techniques, the rewards are still available. There is nothing like eating fresh fish in the middle of winter, and knowing that you caught them with hook and line.

Always use caution when walking on an ice covered pond, and I prefer to always tie a rope around myself and the closest tree…just in case. Fishing in the winter months truly is an experience of a lifetime. Never doubt that Mr. Bass will bite. With the right bait, patience, and determination he will be on your line in no time!

Livestock must be tended to during the winter months. Fresh water must be given daily, as well as a shelter and warmth. Hay can be purchased, or cultivated during the summer months from your land. One will find that off-grid living opens up your door to a host of animals on extremely cold nights. Note: Baby goats are a blast inside.

If you have livestock, hay is essential on your homestead. Small bales, large bales, size does not matter. Contact a local farmer to see if they are willing to sell a few bales. Make arrangements to assist the farmer during hay season as a means of bartering for the hay. Most farmers gladly welcome a helping hand.

Hay, or straw, is also needed to provide bedding for animals, and can be used as insulation surrounding a greenhouse. I place straw bales on the north end of my greenhouse to protect from the cold north winds during the winter.

For those that care to research, winter is also the perfect time to construct an ice house made from straw bales. Cutting your ice during winter and storing it in a well-constructed ice house will ensure fresh ice during the spring and summer months.

EVENING TIME

Evening Time can be best summed up by saying "Quality Family Time." How long has it been since you quietly read a book without interruption? Rocked back and forth on a front porch while enjoying the sounds of nature? Spent an evening playing a board game with family or friends? Quietly sat and sipped a cup of coffee, and just pondered on how wonderful life is?

Reading about games that pioneer families played to pass the time can be very enlightening, and one can see how simple games were a valued part of the family structure. Games brought families together and created times of laughter and bonding. At present, you very seldom hear of the close bond that once held a family together.

Some examples of games played by families in the days past were as simple as a game called "Hull Gull." Everyone would gather and simply take a number of walnuts that the family had collected together, into their hand. It was as simple as guessing how many nuts were being concealed in the hand. How simple is that? I imagine a pioneer family playing this game, and can almost hear the laughter and fun that they had together.

Another game that occupied people for many hours was that of checkers. Now imagine yourself building your own checker board, and then using that board for hours and hours of fun. Are you starting to see the appreciation factor that seems to no longer exists in modern society?

THE VERSATILE 5 GALLON BUCKET

I was asked why I put this chapter towards the end of the book, and my answer is simple, "because I cannot stress enough the importance of 5 gallon buckets." In my opinion, you cannot ever have enough of them. During your initial days of planning, begin collecting 5 gallon buckets.

These little pieces of plastic gold are invaluable on the homestead. One can store and protect food storage; use for a washing machine; carry water; use as a feed bucket; use as a stool; utilize as a chicken nesting box; gardening; hydroponics; rainwater collection, the possibilities are endless.

FURRY FRIENDS

No matter what you do, where you live, how much you try and prevent them from coming, they will always appear on the home homestead. I'm talking about the friendly, and some not so friendly, little furry creatures that just love to see a new homesteader arrive.

I can hear them talking amongst themselves now, "Hey I wonder if they remember to shut their doors?" "How many goodies are inside that wood house?" "Wow, they left me a fresh meal just sitting on the porch!" "How about that feed bag just sitting there waiting for me to eat it?"

Though some see them as pests, and intrusive, I have always enjoyed my little furry friends. They were here first, whether you like it or not. You invaded their world, not the other way around. I take all measures to build them shelters on my property, and provide sources of food during the harsh winter months.

My wife and I actually had a cougar that enjoyed sleeping on top of our cabin. The heat from the woodstove kept the roof warm, and that is where he liked to sleep. I recall the first night he arrived and climbed up onto the roof (We won't reveal that I almost had a small heart attack – that will come in my next book.) But as time has passed, it has come to be just a common thing at my homestead. He presented no threat to my livestock, nor ever bothered my wife or me. It was decided to just leave him be and let him enjoy the homestead as much as we do. His presence does detour a lot of uninvited guests, so it's a win – win situation.

Another animal that is commonly viewed as "worthless" is my Old friend, Mr. Opossum. Opossums eat fruits, snakes (opossums are immune to all types of snake venom, except that of the coral snake), insects, snails, slugs, eggs, mice, rats, fish, frogs, crayfish, and carrion. If for no other reason than pest control, opossums are great to have around!

We had a baby opossum that each night would come up on the porch to eat her dog food. She was not afraid, nor did she make any indication that she would harm the livestock. For those that will raise chickens, all you have to do is build a secure pen. A plus is to feed any opossum visitor a little dog food to offset its natural hunger. Living in harmony with the "critters" can be achieved. It's up to you to decide how to do so.

Another favorite "critter" is Mr. Raccoon. Yes, they are ornery, curious, little packages of destruction, but they are easily tamed to coexist, and offer hours of laughter by just watching them.

For those that like to trap, or hunt raccoon, controlling the population on your homestead is much better than seeing them killed on a roadway due to overpopulation. They also are a formidable opponent. Those little fingers and hands have been known to frustrate even the best trapper.

My wife holding one of our favorite "critters.

Coyotes present a different challenge to the homestead. I have battled with packs of coyotes that constantly wanted to kill my goat herd. One simple mistake and the goats would have been history. Though they still should be afforded the same respect as any other wildlife, please note that they pose a high risk to all livestock and pets that are present on the homestead.

Population control measures must be conducted, and it is my advice to contact your local game warden in order to see how this is to be completed. Normally with a high coyote population, you will not be the only person effected and making inquiry.

Another "critter" that I love to have around my homestead is the beautiful Red Fox. Though they do pose a threat towards chickens on your homestead, this can be controlled by means of an adequate chicken pen. Once completed, you will find that having a red fox in the vicinity is truly a pleasurable experience, especially if they give birth and have babies. To watch a mother fox with her cubs is an experience of a lifetime.

Are you seeing the correlation between your actions and what the friendly "critters" do yet? If you build a secure pen; secure your trash; not leave meat hanging in a tree; then your visitors will truly never impose, nor cause you harm. Then you can simply enjoy their presence.

A SIGH OF SATISFACTION

Once settled onto your new homestead, there is no price that can be placed on the satisfaction you will feel after each day has concluded. Whether it be a day building a livestock pen, or simply just collecting wild flowers, each day can always end in a positive manner. Your happiness is entirely up to you.

Every day you will add or subtract from your homestead. Every day you will face a new challenge that can be overcame with a little imagination and creativity. Nothing in life is easy, but it can be made simpler. Hard work on a homestead will return rewards beyond measure. It is up to you to seek out what you desire; what you hold dear; and what you want for yourself and your family.

Let no person be the reason for you to fail. A homestead is forgiving, and for every failure there is always tomorrow. Nothing is black and white, and nothing is an absolute. You control your destiny...only you.

To close, please remember that life is a gift. Enjoy every second of it, but most of all have fun, smile, and enjoy...

Living with the Critters!